A souvenir guide

# Belton House

## Lincolnshire

MW00332943

**National Trust**

# Interpreting Belton

**With so much history, so many interesting characters, such wonderful collections and views, it's not surprising Belton has been described as the 'perfect' English country house estate.**

Each year the property highlights a different aspect of Belton's history. In 'From Dawn to Dusk', visitors to the house got a real feel for how the different rooms were used throughout the day. The 75th anniversary of the abdication crisis was marked with 'Abdication Hits Home', which focused on Belton in the late 1930s and the role Lord Brownlow played as confidant to Edward VIII. For 'Beyond Face Value', attention turned to Belton's vast array of collections, from veteran trees in the park and tropical planting in the Orangery, to silver, ceramics, paintings and books in the house. 'Belton by Design' saw a focus on aspects of design and designers, both in the house and on the wider estate.

There is so much to Belton and this book can only give you an overview of the highlights. We hope you will find it interesting and that you will want to discover more about the history, people, collections and stories that make up this wonderful estate.

Left Belton's imposing north front

Below Detail of a chest in the Marble Hall inscribed 'Belton House' with an interlocking 'B' symbol

# The People of Belton

Ever since Richard Brownlow acquired the manor at Belton in 1609, successive generations have shaped the estate you see today. The following pages focus on just some of the key family members who left a lasting impression on Belton.

## The first Brownlow at Belton

Richard Brownlow (1553–1638) was a hugely successful lawyer and laid the foundations for the Brownlow family's wealth. In 1591 he was appointed to the important and very lucrative post of Chief Prothonotary of the Court of Common Pleas, with a spectacular salary of £6,000 a year (£18 million in today's money).

He made good use of his wealth and invested heavily in land (sometimes as much as two-thirds of his annual income), with many of his purchases being in Lincolnshire. It is said he caused resentment amongst local landowners, with the short-tempered and impoverished 2nd Earl of Lincoln condemning him as a 'villayne' who 'purchased land every day from under his nose'.

## The birth of the Belton House estate

In 1603 Richard Brownlow began to negotiate with Henry Pakenham for the manor at Belton. Richard was looking for income-generating land rather than a country seat and it is unlikely that the manor house (thought to have been located near the site of the current Orangery) was of any real interest. Brownlow finally bought Belton in 1609 for £4,100 (£11.4 million today) on the agreement that Pakenham and his wife could remain there until their deaths. However, they later became

Above Richard Brownlow, English School, 1624

Right The Church seen from the Italian Garden; its tower was rebuilt by Richard Brownlow in 1638

Above **The Brownlow coat of arms on the south pediment**

impoverished and left in 1619, with Brownlow agreeing to pay them an annuity of £560 during their lifetimes – Pakenham died a year later, but his wife lived on for another 22 years.

The Brownlows rarely visited Belton, preferring to live in London. Beyond acquiring the estate, their ownership had little impact on Belton. Richard's only known architectural legacy is the church tower that he rebuilt in 1638, the year of his death.

Richard's eldest son John died young and so the estate passed to his second son Anthony, who was renamed John. John, (who became known as 'Old' Sir John in order to distinguish him from 'Young' Sir John who followed him and built the present house) inherited the bulk of the family estates, including Belton.

# 'Young' Sir John, the builder of Belton

'Young' Sir John (1659–97) changed the face of Belton. He inherited the estate from his great uncle 'Old' Sir John after the latter outlived his heirs. With an inheritance of £20,000 and an income of around £9,000 a year (£43.9 million and £19.8 million in today's money), he launched himself into society, buying a London home in what is now Bloomsbury Square, before turning his thoughts to the creation of a country house estate.

It is thought that 'Young' Sir John asked soldier-turned-architect William Winde (c.1642–1772) to design his new house. Documents in the family archives suggest the project was supervised by the master mason William Stanton (1639–1705). Stanton was predominantly a sculptor and probably came to 'Young' Sir John's attention when he created the monument to 'Old' Sir John and his wife Alice in Belton church. Between 1685 and 1688 Stanton and his assistant received £5,000 at Belton. This large sum suggests they played a central role in the organisation of the plans and the construction of the house.

Below Architect William Winde was influenced by Roger Pratt's design for Clarendon House, shown here, when he designed Belton House

### Source of inspiration
The design owes something to Roger Pratt as it draws influences from his design for Clarendon House (1664–67) in London, which was described as '… the best contriv'd, the most usefull, gracefull, and magnificent house in England. Here is state and use, solidity and beauty, most symmetrically combined together'. Pratt, amongst others, introduced this predominantly Dutch form of design (an ordered house, topped by balustrades and cupola) into English architecture at this time.

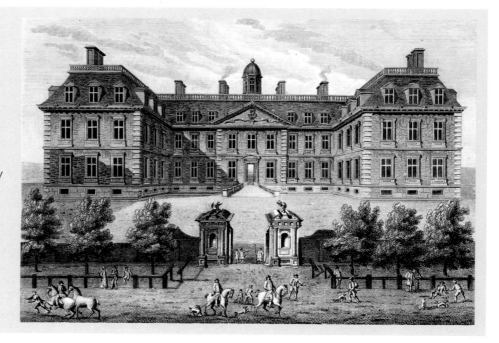

Above *Sir John Brownlow, 'Young' Sir John*
by John Riley and John Closterman, *c.*1685

Above *Alice Sherard, Lady Brownlow* by John Riley and John Closterman,
*c.*1685. Alice stayed at Belton for another 24 years after the death of
'Young' Sir John

## Building commences

Work started on the house in early 1684 as in February kilns and temporary structures were built on site. The old manor was dismantled and the wood, stone, glass, lead and slate stored away for later use. Ringston Hall (former home of 'Young' Sir John's father) was also dismantled and provided 289 loads of stone, slate and wood that were carted 12 miles to Belton. The house was dressed with Ancaster stone from a quarry four miles away at Heydour, while the quoins and keystones came from Stamford.

## An orderly layout

The domestic areas were in the basement, leaving the two main floors free for the family and state apartments. The servant accommodation was in the attics and reached by sets of stairs at either end of the house.

The design of the house focused on four central rooms – the Marble Hall, the Great Parlour (now the Saloon), the Great Dining Room (now the Library) and the State Bedroom and Closet (now the Queen's Bedroom and Ante-Library). The other rooms were placed symmetrically around this inner

Above The Staircase Hall

Opposite top left The Chapel is a superb example of Caroline decoration

Opposite top right The Chapel's delicate ceiling is by noted plasterworker Edward Goudge. Belton's architect William Winde described him as 'the best master in England in his profession'

Opposite below Charles II by Peter Lely, (1618–80)

core, apart from the staircase which was off-set to the east of the Marble Hall in the Little Marble Hall (known as the Staircase Hall from 1830). However, the ceiling by Goudge more than made up for the loss of symmetry and the space was used as a recreational area (complete with billiard table according to the 1688 inventory), a picture gallery and as the ceremonial route to the Great Dining Room above.

The two wings contained nurseries for Brownlow's daughters and rooms for Lady Brownlow's relations to the south and a kitchen and chapel to the north. The Chapel and its adjacent Drawing Room are worthy of special note as they are the least altered of the 17th-century interiors at Belton.

## Fashionable interiors

The 1688 inventory suggests that Belton was furnished in a fairly simple but modern style. The Marble Hall had an amazing 28 paintings of kings and queens as well as the marble floor you see today and was designed as a grand introduction to the rest of the house. Some of the wood carvings are by the aptly named Edmund Carpenter whilst others, lacking supporting documentary evidence, have been attributed to Grinling Gibbons. Whilst they were in the house when it was first built (probably originally in the Great Parlour), they have been rearranged and moved between rooms several times throughout the years.

By 1697, 'Young' Sir John and Lady Brownlow had invested heavily in more fashionable and opulent furnishings for their new home, such as the tapestries (still in the Chapel Drawing Room) commissioned from John Vanderbank (Chief Arras Worker of the Great Wardrobe) which were copies of ones owned by the Queen at Kensington Palace. The inventory also refers to newly named rooms that suggest much more lavish decoration, such as a 'green damask drawing room', a 'white gilt closet' and a 'Scotch plaid room'.

## The Park

The park was enclosed in 1688 after permission was obtained from William III. The King was entertained at Belton during his

Above left Limewood carving thought to be by master carver Grinling Gibbons in the Marble Hall

Above The tapestries in the Chapel Drawing Room were designed by John Vanderbank, whose London workshop was the leading English tapestry manufactory in the late 17th century

and impressive sequence of house, gardens, avenues, formal plantations and parkland. He had also served as High Sheriff for Lincolnshire and MP for Grantham and had entertained the King at Belton.

On 'Young' Sir John's death, Belton passed to his brother William. William died four years later and his eldest son John (who had married 'Young' Sir John's daughter Eleanor) inherited Belton in 1702.

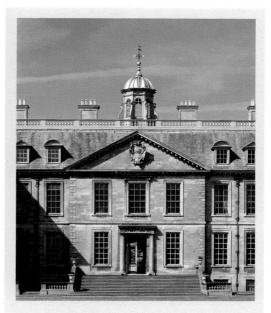

**William Winde**
Although we do not know for sure, it is thought that Captain William Winde (c.1645–1722) designed Belton as it has similarities with his work on Coombe Abbey in Warwickshire. The proportions, pediments, cartouches and window detailing all suggest a common designer. A number of the craftsmen who worked at Belton, such as Edward Goudge who was responsible for the Chapel ceiling and Edward Willcox who made the cupola and balustrades, also had strong links to Winde.

Right The south front of Belton – a beautifully proportioned arrangement of classical features

progress through Lincolnshire and the diarist Abraham de la Pryme recorded the killing of '12 fat oxen and 60 sheep beside other victuals for his entertainment…the king was exceedingly merry and drank freely'. 'Young' Sir John was also responsible for planting thousands of trees throughout the estate.

**Lasting legacy**
In 1697 'Young' Sir John died in a shooting accident and despite his relatively early death aged 39, it is said he had done everything expected of a wealthy country gentleman. In a short time he had created an expansive

# Viscount Tyrconnel, the great collector

There appear to have been two sides to Sir John Brownlow (1690–1754), Viscount Tyrconnel. It is said he was a man of driving political ambition, but with few political skills and an inordinately high opinion of his own importance – not shared by his family, colleagues or peers!

He entered parliament as a Whig in 1713 and held seats for both Grantham and Lincolnshire. In 1718 he was created Viscount Tyrconnel and Baron Charleville in the Irish peerage as a reward for supporting the government, but he never managed to achieve his ultimate ambition of an English peerage. He continued to sit in the Commons as an Irish peer, but made little impression before he retired in 1741.

## An eye for art

He may not have made an impact in the political world, but Belton owes a lot to Tyrconnel. Whilst he may have lacked political prowess, a contemporary is said to have commented on 'his nice taste and his well chosen knowledge' of the arts and it was indeed his artistic taste and knowledge that were to be his greatest legacy.

Right *Sir John Brownlow, Viscount Tyrconnel* by Charles Jervas, 1730s

Belton passed to Tyrconnel and his wife Eleanor in 1721 and became their main residence. They had suffered financial difficulties, partly due to inheriting an encumbered estate and partly from bad financial management, and so began to consolidate their Lincolnshire estates and buy back land that had once belonged to the estate but had been given to Eleanor's sisters. Despite their best efforts, Belton remained a shadow of its former self and only provided them with half the income that 'Old' Sir John had enjoyed in the 17th century. However, the couple were far from poor and Tyrconnel felt free to indulge in the arts. He was inspired by his friend and fellow art lover Frederick, Prince of Wales. The Prince introduced him to painters such as Thomas Smith of Derby and Philippe Mercier as well as the sculptor Henry Cheere and poet Richard Savage.

### 'The Butcher'

Tyrconnel was an ardent anti-Jacobite. In 1746, shortly after the Battle of Culloden, Tyrconnel commissioned a bust of 'Butcher' Cumberland from Henry Cheere. Responsible for putting down the Jacobite Rising, the Duke was for evermore known as 'The Butcher'. The bust was given pride of place in the Marble Hall as a celebration of 'ye News of ye Glorious & Compleat Victory obtain'd over ye Rebels in Scotland'.

Below *Eleanor Brownlow* by Charles Jervas, 1720s

## Grand decorative schemes

We are fortunate to have a number of inventories and bills dating from Tyrconnel's time at Belton. Inventories show that the Saloon (then still known as the Great Parlour) remained a key room and Tyrconnel spent a lot of money on its furnishing and decoration. In 1729 he paid 15 guineas (just over £25,000 today) to have the room gilded and bought 'two large pier glasses with three brass sconces to each' and 'two marble tables'. The pier glasses and tables are still amongst the most important pieces in the house today.

Other significant items include 'two pieces of fine tapestry hangings with the Lord's Arms and history of Diogenes and Plato'. Inventories show that in Tyrconnel's time two of the tapestries hung in what is now the Red Drawing Room. They were part of a set of four tapestries depicting scenes from the life of the philosopher Diogenes and were woven at the Mortlake tapestry factory. It is probable that the other two were kept in Tyrconnel's London home, but the full set are now on display in the Tapestry Room at Belton.

Above The Saloon

Above Detail of the Mortlake tapestry showing an incident from the life of Diogenes

Right One of Tyrconnel's many treasures, this exquisite late 17th-century Italian cabinet is decorated with panels of lapis lazuli and supported by a Charles II giltwood stand

Tyrconnel also worked on several state rooms. In 1742 the ceiling in the Marble Hall was re-plastered (at a cost of £29 17s 4d, nearly £51,000 today) and the following year he paid a further £29 10s 10d (£49,000 today) for work on the staircase ceiling. 'Young' Sir John's bedchamber (now the Queen's Bedroom) was turned into a picture gallery and the 'drawing room next to the great Parlour' (today the Tyrconnel Room) was fitted with a bed of crimson damask, rich furniture, family portraits and ornamental porcelain figures. In 1754 the items in this room were valued at £250 5s (£403,000) making it the most expensively furnished bedroom in the house.

## Beyond the house

In his later years Tyrconnel was also responsible for a number of significant alterations to the grounds which can be seen in the painting by Nollekens dated 1752. He instigated the ha-ha – in place of fencing between the eastern edge of the formal gardens and the park, introduced the 'wilderness' and added several key structures to the grounds such as Bellmount Tower and the Gothick Ruin and Cascade.

## Life and legacy

Despite his refined taste and enthusiasm for learning, Tyrconnel was not admired by all his contemporaries. George II felt he lacked wisdom and principle and called him 'a puppy that never votes twice together on the same side'. Mrs Delany (whom Tyrconnel wooed after Eleanor's death in 1730) wrote that even though 'he had so vast a fortune, a title and was a good natured man . . . money without worth could not tempt her'. He eventually married Elizabeth Cartwright in 1732, but the match was not well received by his family (possibly due to the fact they hoped to see him die childless). In the end the couple did not have children and so turned their attentions and ambitions to those of Tyrconnel's sister Anne, especially her eldest son, John.

It is through Tyrconnel's interest as a patron of the arts that his great legacy comes to us. He started Belton's collections of porcelain, books, silver and pictures. Information on key pieces can be found on pages 34–39.

Left *Belton House and Gardens, A Bird's Eye View* by Nollekens, 1752

Above right This portrait of King George II hangs at Belton. The king criticised Tyrconnel for what he believed was lack of political integrity

Right The Cascade at Belton, as depicted in an 18th-century painting

# Sir John Cust, 'Speaker Cust'

Sir John (1718–70) was the eldest nephew of Viscount Tyrconnel and moved to Grantham with his mother and eight siblings on the death of his father. As Tyrconnel and his wife had no children, they focused their ambitions on their nephews and nieces and Tyrconnel used his influence to advance John's political career. He arranged for his admission to the Middle Temple and used his position to ensure his nephew's election as MP for Grantham in 1739, a seat which he held until his death.

## A distinguished career

Tyrconnel's hopes were well placed and John's career proved to be considerably more distinguished than his uncle's, although Tyrconnel never lived to see the full extent of his achievement. When Tyrconnel died, his sister moved her family into Belton and gave her Grantham house to Sir John; it is said he rarely used it as he spent most of his time in London and stayed with his mother when visiting Lincolnshire.

Sir John was said to be a shrewd diplomat in both politics and his private life. He was appointed Clerk of the Household to the Princess of Wales in 1751, before being elected Speaker of the Commons in 1761. At this point his mother moved back to Grantham House and gave him Belton as she felt the estate was more in keeping with his new position – much to the chagrin of his brothers and sisters!

It is said that Sir John momentarily toyed with the idea of retiring from politics to live the life of a country gentleman, but was re-elected in 1768 and subsequently presided over one of the stormiest periods in British parliamentary history. He died in 1770 aged 51. His monument in Belton church attributes his death to the 'unusual fatigues of his office', brought about by 'the extraordinary increase of national business'.

Cust made little impact on Belton and it was left to his son Brownlow Cust to make the first major architectural changes to the house since it had been built in 1688.

Opposite *The family of Sir Richard and Lady Cust* by Enoch Seeman, 1740s. The widowed Anne Cust sits surrounded by her children. She inherited Belton from her brother, Viscount Tyrconnel, and passed it to her eldest son (who sits next to her) when he became Speaker of the Commons

Left *Portrait of Sir John Cust, 'Speaker Cust'* by Sir Joshua Reynolds, 1767–68

Below Anne Cust returned to live at Grantham House after her son John inherited Belton

# Brownlow, Baron Brownlow, the remodeller

Sir Brownlow Cust (1744–1807) was in a very comfortable position when he inherited Belton in 1770. He had a significant income, thanks to £103,000 (£11 million in today's money) from his first wife Jocosa Drury and £100,000 (£10 million) from his second wife Frances Banks whom he married in 1775. A year later, he was raised to the peerage as a reward for his father's distinguished political service.

The house he inherited must have seemed very old fashioned and he quickly arranged a series of alterations and repairs. Invoices show that within two years of taking up ownership, he had repainted the house, altered architraves and mouldings, repaired floors, replaced windows and redecorated several rooms.

## Following fashion

Brownlow did not, however, just commission decorators. He also instigated far more dramatic alterations. In 1776 he consulted James Wyatt, who was soon to become one of the country's most fashionable designers.

Above *Sir Brownlow Cust, Baron Brownlow* by George Romney, 1780s

Right *Jocosa Katerina Drury, Lady Cust, with her niece Lady Caroline Hobart* by Benjamin West, 1770s

Wyatt's appointment suggests Brownlow was eager to employ an architect who had the vision to transform Belton into a residence befitting a new peer.

Externally, Wyatt erased all traces of the late 17th century. He removed the cupola and balustrades from the roof and retiled it in Westmorland slate. He changed the alternating shapes of the dormer windows and reduced them from eight to six windows on each front. He inserted sash windows in the new dormers and blocked up a number of windows on the south front to create niches. He also designed dramatic new features for the main entrance. His alterations gave Belton the appearance of a Caroline house, remodelled to bring it in line with mid-Georgian taste.

Front of the PANTHEON, OXFORD STREET.

Above Designed by James Wyatt and opened in 1772, the Pantheon was one of London's most famous buildings of the time. Its popularity helped Wyatt gain many commissions, including Belton House

Above right *James Wyatt* by Joseph Singleton, 1795

## James Wyatt

James Wyatt (1746–1813) made a name for himself when, aged just 26, he designed the Pantheon in Oxford Street. This public building quickly became a fashionable place of public entertainment. After his designs for the Pantheon were exhibited at the Royal Academy in 1770, Wyatt was soon overwhelmed with commissions. Horace Walpole called it 'the most beautiful edifice in England'.

Wyatt was probably recommended to Brownlow by Philip Yorke of Erddig, who was married to Brownlow's sister and had worked with Wyatt on alterations to his own house.

It is said that Wyatt had an amazingly cavalier attitude towards his clients and that his lack of organisational skills was legendary – but this didn't stop him from getting more commissions from the aristocracy as well as from King George III. In the latter part of his career Wyatt shifted from a neo-classical style to a fully Gothic one – surviving examples of this can be seen at Ashridge in Hertfordshire and Belvoir Castle in Leicestershire. His work as an interior and furniture designer has been described as a refinement on Robert Adam's famed neo-classical style.

Above One of Wyatt's potential designs for the drawing room ceiling, now the Library

Left The Library

## Wyatt's alterations

Internally, Wyatt redecorated four rooms but only some of his work remains as a number of further alterations came later. On the first floor he changed a bedchamber into a dressing room for Lady Brownlow. The room is now the Boudoir, but it still retains a number of Wyatt's features, such as the delicate cornice freeze and splendid plaster ceiling, and maintains a feminine feel in an otherwise distinctly masculine house. In the room next door, Wyatt transformed the old great chamber into a classical drawing room. Servant quarters in the attics were sacrificed to create a shallow vaulted ceiling with decorative plasterwork. The drawing room was later converted into the Library, but the ceiling survives.

Wyatt also remodelled the Yellow and Blue Bedrooms in the south-east wing. In the Blue Bedroom, Wyatt's delicate cornice frieze, dado and chimneypiece survive, although they are overshadowed by a towering state bed. The bed has a complicated history and it is unlikely to have been part of Wyatt's scheme as he would not have incorporated such a dominant piece of furniture into his design.

Wyatt's remodelling of the first floor Yellow Bedroom is a little more unclear as no mention of it appears in archive material, the only evidence coming from four of his drawings (dated from 1777–8). The drawings show the areas around the windows, chimney and door. On the framing for the door, Wyatt noted that the upper part was to be 'enrich'd the same as

Left The Blue Bedroom

Below Neoclassical
ceiling in the Boudoir

the Great Cornice. Stucco frieze the same as
the Room'. Wyatt was also responsible for
blocking up the four east windows and
opening up the view of the park to the south as
seen in the present window arrangement.

## All change

In addition to Wyatt's work, Brownlow was
busy installing stoves and a water closet in the
house, buying new furniture and adding to an
already distinguished collection of paintings.
He commissioned portraits of both his wives
and purchased thousands of pounds worth of
furniture. By the time of his death in 1807,
Belton had been well and truly dragged into
the 19th century. Its surviving Caroline
decoration may have been still at odds with
the elegance and convenience of its Georgian
interiors, but there were more changes to
come.

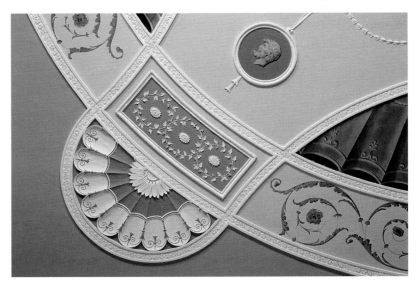

# The 1st Earl, a Renaissance man

A scholarly and cultured man, John Cust (1779–1853), 2nd Baron Brownlow, was created 1st Earl in 1815. He enjoyed the Grand Tour of Europe in 1802 and was patron to a number of contemporary artists, including Antonio Canova and Richard Westmacott. He was also responsible for many of Belton's important collections, most notably the silver and the Italian books.

The 1st Earl grew up at a time of political upheaval in the aftermath of the French Revolution and with the fear of political rebellion at home. He had a strong belief in maintaining social hierarchy and in resisting reform. When the Lords threw out the Reform Bill in 1831, the 1st Earl created a household militia in order to protect Belton from possible attacks by rioters.

## Wyatville designs

The 1st Earl was quick to make his mark on Belton. He employed the services of the architect Jeffry Wyatt (who later changed his name to Wyatville and was the nephew of James Wyatt who had worked for the 1st Earl's father) and brought about real changes in the house and across the estate.

On the estate his work included the Orangery and Lion Exedra in the Italian Garden, the Brew house and refurbished Stable courtyard, as well as a number of cottages and the village smithy. He was also responsible for buildings in the villages of Manthorpe and Londonthorpe.

Within the house, Wyatville's most significant alteration was to the upper part of the old kitchen, which he converted into a new room (now the Hondecoeter or Dining Room) to house the Earl's large collection of books, re-siting the kitchens in the west range. Wyatville also created the Chinese Bedroom, remodelled the Red Drawing Room (introducing heavy gilding and crimson damask), remodelled the doors to the Saloon and Marble Hall, altered the main staircase (creating the white and gold colour scheme you see today) and introduced the rich foliate ceiling rose in the Marble Hall.

Left *John Cust, 1st Earl Brownlow* (1835), by leading society portraitist and president of the Royal Academy, Sir Martin Archer Shee PRA

Opposite top The Chinese Bedroom

Opposite below This 19th-century watercolour shows the rich decorative scheme – combining much use of gilding and crimson damask – that Wyatville introduced into the Red Drawing Room

Below Miniature portrait of Jeffry Wyatville, who is now best known for his remodelling of Windsor Castle

## The Earl's heirs

Although the 1st Earl's son, Viscount Alford, inherited the vast Egerton estates in 1849 (worth £70,000 a year, around £47.6 million today), he predeceased his father by two years and so never inherited Belton.

The 1st Earl died in 1853. The family estates passed to his 11-year-old grandson, John William Egerton Cust (1842–67), whose mother Lady Marian took charge of both Belton and Ashridge (the main Egerton property, in Hertfordshire) until he came of age. However, the 2nd Earl had little chance to make his mark on Belton as he died unmarried at the age of 25. Belton then passed to his brother Adelbert, the charismatic 3rd and last Earl.

# The 3rd Earl, a true Victorian

Known as 'Addy' the 3rd Earl (1844–1921) was a tall and handsome man, unaffected by his position, with wonderful manners and full of stories of his adventures whilst serving abroad in the army. He married Adelaide Talbot (daughter of the 18th Earl of Shrewsbury) in 1868 and it was said they made a striking couple.

There were many sides to Addy and Adelaide. The 3rd Earl entered politics, holding minor office in three Conservative administrations. Locally they played an active and key role in society, with the 3rd Earl taking on the role of Colonel of the local militia and Lord Lieutenant of Lincolnshire. They also moved in intellectual circles and were on the fringes of a group of high-minded, idealistic and intellectual aristocrats known as 'the Souls'.

The couple spent most of their time in London or at Ashridge. However, they also made significant changes to Belton, spending a lot of time and money on remodelling the house to reinstate many of the original features and restore it to its original Caroline appearance. Unlike his forbears, the 3rd Earl was governed by what he felt to be the spirit of Belton, rather than by the latest fashions.

Right *Adelbert Wellington Brownlow Cust, 3rd Earl Brownlow* by Frank O. Salisbury, 1908

Opposite Detail of *Adelaide Talbot, Countess Brownlow* by Frank O. Salisbury, 1908

## Transforming Belton

The 3rd Earl's architect is unknown, but we do know that he worked hard to reinstate the features that had been stripped away a century earlier by James Wyatt and Wyatville (who always spelt his name with a single 't' to disassociate himself from his uncle's – in his eyes – reputation). The roof and dormer window features were reinstated, a new domestic wing was added to link the house to the stable yard, and several rooms were redecorated.

On the ground floor, the Saloon received a new plaster ceiling in the spirit of those created by Edward Goudge. The small dining room was also given a new plaster ceiling and oak panelling and then became the Tapestry Room after Addy and Adelaide rediscovered Tyrconnel's Diogenes Tapestries. One of the most striking changes came with the unusual painted floor in the Tyrconnel Room. The origins of the floor, which shows the 17th-century crest of the Brownlow family, has been the subject of much debate and still divides opinion. They also transformed Wyatville's library into a dining room (now the Hondecoeter or Dining Room).

The conversion of the library into a dining room meant a new room was needed for the large collection of books and a local firm was

Above The Tapestry Room, with its superb Diogenes Tapestries

Opposite above Detail of the painted floor in the Tyrconnel Room. The painted greyhound is a reference to the Brownlow family coat of arms

Opposite below The Dining Room

### Mystery motifs

One of the most striking additions from Addy's time was the unusual painted floor in the Tyrconnel Room. The decoration around the central circle suggests a Greek influence, popular at the time of Wyatville's remodelling. It also echoes the parterres popular at the time of 'Young' Sir John. Current thinking, however, supports the idea that it was introduced as another neo-Caroline imitation or 'pastiche' by the 3rd Earl.

hired to move Wyatville's bookcases to the drawing room on the first floor. They also redecorated the Boudoir, covering the walls with green striped silk but retaining Wyatt's dado, cornice frieze and ceiling. They did not wipe out all traces of the work by Wyatt and Wyatville and their new interiors have since become important historical features in their own right, but they did do more than any other generation to restore the original character of 'Young' Sir John's house.

The 3rd Earl outlived his cousin and intended heir Harry Cust by 4 years. In January 1921 the barony (but not the earldom which became extinct) and estates passed to his younger cousin Adelbert Salusbury Cockayne Cust, who at the age of 54 had never expected to inherit.

# The 5th Baron Brownlow, the consolidator

Adelbert Salusbury Cockayne Cust (1867–1927) never expected to be master of Belton House. He was a great nephew of the 1st Earl and cousin to the 3rd Earl Brownlow and inherited the Brownlow estates and barony on the death of the 3rd Earl in 1921.

Adelbert inherited Belton at a difficult time. The estate's finances were strained, Belton was mortgaged; income from land and rents was dropping and large death duties had to be paid. Adelbert set about consolidating his inheritance. Ashridge in Hertfordshire was sold under the terms of the Earl's will in order to pay death duties, whilst other holdings such as the Cheshire estates and the London house were sold to pay off mortgages. Adelbert turned Belton's fortunes around. Over the next six years he would play an active role in the local community and serve as mayor of Grantham.

## Community work
Maud, Lady Brownlow (1870–1936), married Adelbert in 1895. On becoming mistress of Belton, she supported her husband in all his public works. She would regularly visit the local villagers, enquiring after those who were ill and arranging parcels of milk, eggs and soup for families with newborn babies.

Opposite *Adelbert Salusbury Cockayne Cust, 5th Baron Brownlow* (detail) by Sir Frank O. Salisbury, 1925

Right *Maud Buckle, Lady Brownlow* by Sir Frank O. Salisbury, 1925

# The 6th Baron and the abdication crisis

Peregrine Adelbert Cust (1899–1978) inherited Belton in 1927 and was destined to play a part in history that had repercussions for Belton and the entire country. He is often remembered now, not for the way he sought to preserve Belton, but for his role in the abdication crisis of 1936.

## The King's confidant

Peregrine was a close friend of Edward, Prince of Wales, who occasionally visited Belton. When Edward became king in January 1936, 'Perry' was appointed Lord in Waiting. When rumours spread of the King's intentions to marry Wallis Simpson his advisors put pressure

Below left *Peregrine Adelbert Cust, 6th Baron Brownlow* by Edward I Halliday, 1956

Below right *Katherine Kinloch, Lady Brownlow* by Simon Elwes, 1939

**Daily Express**

TODAY'S WEATHER: MILDER. TUESDAY, DECEMBER 8, 1936 ONE PENNY

164 PAGES of Good Advice

No. 11,409

*Mrs. Simpson Authorises*
*Dramatic Statement From Cannes*

M WILLING TO WITHDRAW

ch Action Would Solve The Problem

LATEST NEWS
Telephone: Central 8000

D BROWNLOW
EADS SIGNED
DOCUMENT

ation Which Has Become
Unhappy And Untenable'

Daily Express Staff Reporter

CANNES, Monday Night.
mpson is "willing, if such action would solve
em, to withdraw forthwith from a situation
been rendered both unhappy and untenable."
er is made in a statement signed by Mrs. Simpson herself
Brownlow, Lord-in-Waiting to and close friend of the King.
ress Conference in the Hotel Majestic, Cannes, tonight. The
aid:—
. Simpson, throughout the last few

Above Front page of
the *Daily Express*, dated
8 December 1936. Edward
VIII abdicated two days
later

Right *Edward John
Peregrine Cust, 7th Baron
Brownlow* by Howard
Morgan, 1988

on her to leave the country. Peregrine was
concerned that if she left, the King would
follow her and force the abdication they
were all seeking to avoid. Peregrine tried to
persuade Wallis to come to Belton so that
she could prevent the King from doing
anything hasty.

On 3 December the crisis appeared in the
press. Prime Minister Stanley Baldwin
announced that the government could not
approve of the marriage or the suggestion that
Edward could marry Mrs Simpson without
making her Queen. The King left London for
Windsor and Peregrine took Wallis to Cannes
to wait for the crisis to blow over. Perry
pressured Wallis to give up the King and on
7 December she made a statement saying that
she would withdraw. Perry advised her on the
wording and read the statement to the press.

On 10 December 1936 at 3.55pm the Prime
Minister read Edward's letter of abdication to
the House of Commons. The King broadcast

his now famous farewell speech that evening
and left England the next day. Perry, amongst
other advisors, was blamed for the whole affair
and the Archbishop of Canterbury accused
them of 'consuming' Edward and leading him
to his downfall.

Perry retreated from public life and Belton
remained much as it had when he inherited it.
However, by the 1960s the house was in need of
urgent repair and a major programme of work
was carried out with grant-aid from the Historic
Buildings Council. The roof was re-slated,
leading replaced, serious dry rot was tackled,
panelling was taken down and repaired,
cornices were replaced and a number of rooms
redecorated. Perry opened Belton to the public
once this work had been completed.

### The gift of Belton

The 6th Baron died in 1978 and six years
later his son Edward gave Belton House, its
garden and some of its contents to the
National Trust. In addition the Trust
bought parkland and many of the
remaining contents and set up an
endowment to help maintain the property.
The total cost of £8 million was met by a
combination of bequests to the National
Trust and a grant from the National
Heritage Memorial Fund.

# The Collections

Despite successive sales in the early 20th century, Belton has retained indigenous collections of such diversity, splendour and in some cases rarity, that it truly can be called one of the National Trust's great treasure houses.

In every corner there are wonderful objects to discover, collected over successive generations and recognised as great examples of their kind – from masterpieces by artists such as Frederic, Lord Leighton and Philippe Mercier to rare Chinese and Sèvres porcelain.

# Collection highlights: Portraits

Belton House is particularly notable for its collection of portraits which include works by Mercier, Kneller, Leighton, Salisbury, Reynolds, Watts and Romney. Having your portrait painted showed the world you had arrived – position, possessions, wealth and land could be celebrated for all to see.

*Lady Adelaide Chetwynd-Talbot, Countess Brownlow* (c.1879) by Frederic, Lord Leighton PRA

This is perhaps Leighton's finest female portrait and was exhibited at the Royal Academy in 1879. Painted at Ashridge Park (Hertfordshire) it depicts Lady Brownlow, daughter of the 18th Earl of Shrewsbury.

Adelaide married the 3rd Earl Brownlow in 1868 and they spent most of their time at Ashridge Park or their London house in Carlton House Terrace. They did, however, take a great interest in Belton, reinstating some of the 17th-century features lost through previous generations and so restoring its original splendour.

*Lord and Lady Tyrconnel in the Park at Belton,*
*also known as 'The Belton Conversation Piece'*
*c.1724–6) by Philippe Mercier*

In a house full of masterpieces by some of
history's great portrait painters, this piece is
till considered by many to be the outstanding
painting in the collection.

Prior to the mid-18th century, portraits were
very formal and poses were classical in style,
making much of drapery, pillars and sculpture.

The arrival of Philippe Mercier from France
changed all that. He started to paint what
became known as 'conversation pieces'.
*Lord and Lady Tyrconnel in the Park* at Belton
(now in the Breakfast Room) shows this
more informal style, a lady on a swing

and even the family pet! This depiction of
the family 'at play' changed the art of
portraiture forever.

Mercier's finest painting shows Lord
Tyrconnel standing to the left of the picture
watching the artist painting the scene.
Lady Tyrconnel sits in a wheelchair with other
family members gathered around. This
painting marks a change in portrait painting;
the sitters are no longer just sitting, they
appear to be interacting with each other and in
the case of the figure on the far right (thought
to be Tyrconnel's brother William) even
interacting with the viewer. The inclusion of
the artist in such an intimate scene is also a
rarity, perhaps a symbol of the patronage
Tyrconnel gave to the arts.

# Collection highlights: Porcelain

**The porcelain at Belton is considered to be an excellent cross-section of the sort you would hope to find in a house of this size and date. It is representative of each generation and reflects the changing tastes of English porcelain collecting.**

The objects chosen here represent the three main collectors of porcelain at Belton: the Blanc-de-Chine is from the time of 'Young' Sir John, the composite vase reflects the tastes of Viscount Tyrconnel and the Sèvres is from the 1st Earl.

**Blanc-de-Chine flared beakers, 1600–44**
These beakers are amongst our earliest examples of Chinese porcelain and date from the Ming dynasty. They give us an idea of the fine white translucent wares that had been admired for centuries, before the introduction into China of the blue and white decoration which we now more readily associate with Chinese porcelain.

**Black Sèvres, *c*.1780**
This is one of seven pieces of very rare black Sèvres porcelain, featuring black and gold chinoiserie decoration. This form of porcelain was not produced in large amounts and it is unclear how these rare items came to be at Belton House.

The factories at Sèvres trace their roots back to Lille and Rouen, before moving to Paris in 1738. King Louis XV became a key shareholder in the company and moved it in 1756 to the suburb of Sèvres, from where the company takes its name. At the time this object was made, Sèvres was the pre-eminent porcelain manufacturer in Europe. Despite almost going out of business only a decade later, it still survives today and produces high quality contemporary porcelain.

**Composite vase, *c*.1700**
This vase is characteristic of the 'China mania' that swept through English society during this period. There was a fashion at the time for assembling amusing combinations of oriental porcelain and this very rare composite of three vases is a great example. Assembled in Europe around 1700, it comprises three oriental vases. The bottom storage jar with a courtyard scene and the top triple gourd bottle are both Chinese *c*.1690, whilst the central baluster jar with landscape scene is Japanese *c*.1680.

# Collection highlights: Silver

**For centuries, the beauty, lustre and intrinsic value of silver has made it the perfect way to demonstrate wealth, power and status. Belton's silver embodies the official and personal high points in the history of the family.**

**Set of four William and Mary oval pilgrim bottles (*c.*1690)**
These pilgrim bottles are the most important surviving pieces of 'Young' Sir John's display plate. They are vast and were very expensive, although the form is derived from the humble leather water pouch used by travellers.

While the decorative work on the neck of these wonderful silver gilt bottles is original, dating to the early years of the house and to 'Young' Sir John himself, the decoration on the bodies and the coat of arms date from the early 19th century and were most likely commissioned by the 1st Earl Brownlow. Items such as these were intended to demonstrate the high status of the owner. However silver gilt (a thin layer of gold on top of silver) also has a practical quality. Citrus fruits can cause plain silver to tarnish, but by adding a thin layer of gold to dessert cutlery and dishes this problem could be avoided.

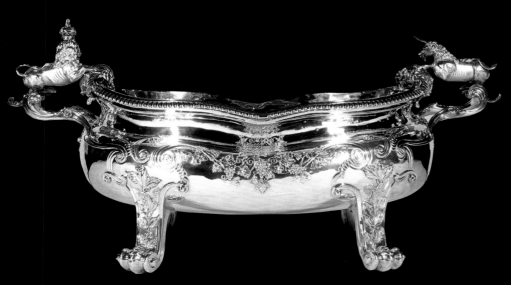

## Wine cistern (1770) by Thomas Hemming

Sir John Cust (or 'Speaker Cust') was elected MP for Grantham in 1739. The silver collection was transformed when he became Speaker in 1761. On gaining office, the Speaker was issued with 4,000 ounces (113.4kg) of silver plate intended for official use. Sir John held the office twice.

The most spectacular item from this period is the wine cistern, commissioned as part of a second allocation of silver following Sir John's re-election in 1768. It was ordered in 1769 but did not arrive until after the Speaker's death. The body is engraved on one side with the royal arms of George III, whilst the other side has the arms of Sir John with royal supporters of a lion and a unicorn creating the handles. Containing 1,457 ounces (41.3kg) of silver, this is a late example of a cistern and was probably intended for show rather than practical use.

## Infantryman of the 11th Division (1915) by Elkington and Co

This silver figure of an infantryman was presented to the 3rd Earl and Countess Brownlow in 1915 by the regiments that had camped and trained on Belton Park before leaving for the front lines in July the same year.

Three months later, in October 1915, the Machine Gun Corps was formed on Belton Park. Over the next six years approximately 175,000 officers and men would be housed and trained at Belton.

The plinth is engraved with this presentation inscription:

| 33rd Brigade | 32nd Brigade | 34th Brigade |
|---|---|---|
| 6th Batt Lincs Reg | 6th Batt East Yorks Reg | 8th Batt N'umberland Reg |
| 6th Batt Border Reg | 9th Batt West Yorks Reg | 9th Batt Lincolnshire Reg |
| 7th Batt 8th Staffs Reg | 8th Batt Yorks Reg | 5th Batt Dorset Reg |
| 9th Batt Notts & Derby Reg | 8th Batt West Riding Reg | 11th Batt Manchester Reg |
| | 6th Batt York & Lancs Reg | |

# The Gardens

Left *The Prospect of Belton* by Philippe Mercier shows the grounds at Belton in the mid-18th century

Opposite Masses of daffodils edge the Statue Walk in spring

## 'Young' Sir John's garden

The engraving by Hendrik Hulsbergh for Colen Campbell's *Vitruvius Britannicus* (1717) shows 'Young' Sir John's very formal plans for parterres and walks. Also visible is a bowling green, kitchen garden, orchards and an obelisk or fountain.

The plan also shows the Great Pond which lay to the east of the house that now looks towards Bellmount Tower. In this area there was also a raised flower garden with access into the Chapel Drawing Room. The garden and park were all enclosed by a five-mile wall in 1690.

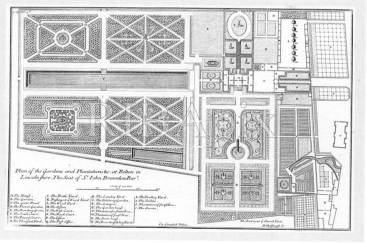

# A brief history

'Young' Sir John was as interested in the design of the grounds at Belton as he was his new house. The house was built in 1684–8, but in 1685 alone he planted nearly 40,000 trees!

As with interiors, garden designs go in and out of fashion. When Viscount Tyrconnel inherited Belton he installed a heated greenhouse and created the Wilderness, Cascade and Gothick Ruin in keeping with the fashion of the time.

The 1st Baron Brownlow employed the landscape gardener William Emes (1729–1803) to draw up a 'Plan of the park and of the Demesne lands at Belton … with some Alterations'. Emes suggested an open pleasure ground surrounded by serpentine walks and woodland and an Orangery to the east of the house. Many of these ideas did not come to fruition, although a pleasure ground was created.

The 1st Earl was responsible for the Italian Garden and Orangery, and the Boathouse and Cascade in the Pleasure Grounds. The 3rd Earl was mainly concerned with restoring many of Belton's Caroline features, but he did also create the Dutch garden.

During the war, large areas of the gardens were used to grow fruit and vegetables to support the war effort. The pergola and the maze were also removed at this time.

Since Belton came to the National Trust in 1984, a maze has been recreated, the Orangery has been repaired, the Statue Walk has been reinstated, the Boathouse has been restored and the Cascade and walkway to the lake have been uncovered and re-established. The gardens at Belton have developed over time and their formal and informal areas are now enjoyed by thousands of people each year.

# The Italian Garden

You would not know to look at it today, but this area was originally part of the kitchen garden. In 1816 the 1st Earl asked Jeffry Wyatville to remodel this area as it had been destroyed by a flood years earlier. Wyatville's plans included the Orangery, fountain, Lion Exedra, trellises and two aviaries.

The Orangery is thought to stand on the site of the former manor house. When it was built in 1820, the Orangery was at the cutting edge of design. It has an internal cast iron supporting structure and an artificial stone roof balustrade. The roof statues were added in 1890.

The fountain was powered from the pump house by the Cascade and Gothick Ruin (the later water wheel and pump were restored in 2011). The Lion Exedra (also by Wyatville,

Above The Fountain and Lion Exedra in the Italian Garden

Opposite The Orangery houses a wide variety of tropical plants and ferns

with lion mask by Richard Westmacott) was moved to its present position in 1921.

The 3rd Earl added box-edged parterres to what became known as the Italian Garden and a cast-iron, ivy-covered pergola was installed around the fountain. On either side of the Orangery were trellises, a parterre and a series of small beds. They were edged with box and planted with violas.

## Blooming border

The Herbaceous border contains a variety of climbing plants as well as a cut flower border which still produces blooms for the house. South facing, it is a riot of colour from early summer until late autumn. The interesting trees are Nottingham Medlars. Here you can also still see the original gate to the manor house.

# The Dutch Garden

Created in 1879, the Dutch Garden is part of the 3rd Earl's neo-Caroline 'restoration' of Belton. The garden takes its name from a strictly geometric style that favoured formal parterres divided by gravelled paths and topiary and was introduced from Holland in the late 17th century. The Dutch Garden was originally designed with parterres and 40 flowerbeds filled with spring blossoms (as the 3rd Earl visited Belton in the spring each year). The golden and Irish yews were planted when the garden was laid out, as were the clipped yew hedges which surround it.

Today, the garden incorporates large beds of lavender, which look and smell glorious during the summer months. The parterres retain their golden and Irish yews, whilst the garden also contains beds with seasonal planting.

## Moondial

The sundial was made famous by the children's author Helen Cresswell who wrote her book, *Moondial*, after being inspired by a visit to Belton. The book has since been adapted for television and many schools visit Belton each year to re-enact the story and see the Moondial for themselves. The Moondial is actually a limestone sundial showing Eros (Greek god of Love) and Cronos (Greek god also known as Father Time), carved by Caius Gabriel Cibber, 'sculptor in ordinary to His Majesty William III'. It was introduced to the garden by Viscount Tyrconnel.

# The Pleasure Grounds

Pleasure Grounds, wide expanses of grass surrounded by trees and enclosed by a ha-ha (a form of sunken fence), were very popular in the mid- to late 18th century and were proposed by William Emes as part of his redesign for the park and gardens at Belton.

Originally 'Young' Sir John had pursued a more formal style for the gardens when he began redesigning Belton as his perfect country house estate. In 1685 alone, he planted 21,400 ash trees, 9,500 oaks, 614 fruit trees, 260 limes, 2,000 roses and 100 gooseberry bushes!

The Pleasure Grounds at Belton retain a little of their original design and feature substantial shrubberies incorporating box, hollies, lilac and azaleas. The oldest surviving tree is the beech by the Mirror Pond. The planting in this section is more natural and the area is particularly striking in spring (when the family were traditionally in residence) with magnificent displays of snowdrops, primroses, cowslips, aconites, daffodils and bluebells.

Above right View of Belton House in April across the Mirror Pond

Right Children enjoying the view from the restored Boathouse

Opposite top The Boathouse in 1908

Opposite below Architectural drawing of the Boathouse by Anthony Salvin

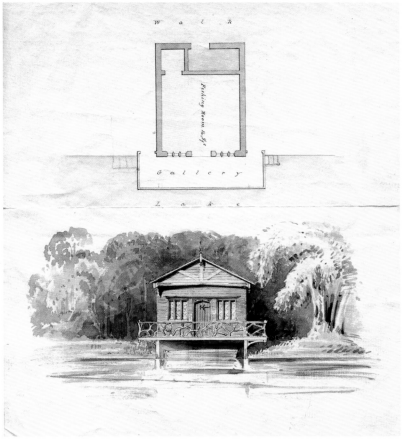

## By the lake

The far end of the Pleasure Grounds features more informal planting. There are paths leading to the Boathouse and a circular lakeside walk. Archaeology revealed a series of terraces near the lakeshore dating back to the 1820s. The garden team have recreated the terraces and the original approach to the Boathouse which offers views of the lake, Bellmount Tower and surrounding parkland. The Boathouse was used by the family for private picnics and fishing parties; today it is a wonderfully tranquil area in which to enjoy a walk or watch wildlife. Along the north boundary is a shelter belt, a long wind break protecting the planted areas.

**Beautiful boathouse**
Designed by Anthony Salvin in 1821 in the Swiss chalet style, the Boathouse was to be the centrepiece of the Pleasure Grounds. It was the ideal place for the Brownlows to picnic and enjoy their estate.

# The Park

The park at Belton is a classic example of English parkland. It was first enclosed in 1690 after 'Young' Sir John Brownlow gained royal approval for a deer park from William III.

Although it looks natural, as with many country house estates, it is in fact a designed landscape. Between 1742 and 1751 Viscount Tyrconnel commissioned William Emes to redesign the surrounding parkland. William Emes incorporated the existing ancient woodland and areas of pasture into his design, as well as creating new vistas featuring ponds, a picturesque 'wilderness' and the Bellmount Tower. The River Witham, which cuts across the edge of the park, did not escape the redesign; a dam was introduced in order to create a cascade water feature to complement the Gothick Ruin.

The 1st Lord Brownlow established plantations on the south side of the park and changed the main approach from the South Avenue to a new road to the east connecting the estate with the village. By the time of his death in 1807, the park looked much as it does today. The South Avenue eventually became a private road to the house and new public roads were built along the boundaries.

More recent additions or alterations to the park include the Alford Memorial in 1852 which was commissioned by the 1st Earl in memory of his son and heir Viscount Alford; the golf course laid out by the 3rd Earl in 1892; evidence of the Machine Gun Corps training camp from 1915–20; and the felling and subsequent replanting of the South Avenue in the 1970s due to Dutch elm disease.

Below The Alford Memorial was built by the 1st Earl in 1852 in memory of his son who died aged 39

The Bellmount Tower consists of a tall arch supporting two rooms reached by a spiral staircase. Situated at the end of the East Avenue, it served both as a focal point and viewing tower

## The park today

In 1984 the National Trust took ownership of Belton House and bought the surrounding parkland. Today, it has a dual purpose as a haven for wildlife and the Trust's only naturally maintained deer park whilst also functioning as a 'green lung' for the ever expanding town of Grantham. It plays host to prestigious events such as the Belton horse trials and also offers a big open natural space for people to explore every day of the year.

# A park rich in wildlife

Belton's herd of around 300 fallow deer are direct descendants of the wild herd first enclosed by 'Young' Sir John in 1690. They have large, flat antlers and come in four colour variations: menil (pale), melanistic or black, 'common' (tan or fawn with white spots) and white. The young are born in June and then hidden in the grass by their mothers to protect them from predators.

Whilst Belton's deer herd enjoys a relatively high profile, the park also provides habitats for a wide range of lesser-seen yet important wildlife. Brown long-eared, Daubenton's, pipistrelle, whiskered, noctule and Natterer's bats have all made their home in the park and are thriving. Brown long-eared bats use the Bellmount Tower as a maternity roost.

Below Young male deer in Belton Park, with the Bellmount Tower in the background

The nocturnal white-clawed crayfish is another protected species thriving at Belton. In fact, the River Witham is the only area in Lincolnshire to still have a native population. White-clawed crayfish are under threat nationally from mink, poor water quality and crayfish plague (a disease brought in by imported American or Signal crayfish). In order to ensure their protection, the wardens at Belton have created a crayfish sanctuary in one of the park ponds.

Water voles are yet another species flourishing in Belton Park whilst rapidly declining elsewhere due to the loss of their natural habitats and an increase in the mink population. Somewhat ironically it is human interference that has actually helped the water voles. When the river was dammed as part of the park's redesign, it also had an effect on the water levels in the river. The dam means less fluctuation in the water levels and the burrows do not flood, creating very favourable conditions for the water voles.

Above left The Natterer's bat often roosts in old buildings and barns in the summer months

Above The white-clawed crayfish only has white undersides; seen from above it is completely brown

Below Water voles prefer calm or still water as a habitat

# Belton Park and the Machine Gun Corps

**In 1915 the park underwent a dramatic makeover when it became home to the newly formed Machine Gun Corps (MGC).**

Belton Park has a long history of military connections and archaeologists have uncovered a number of finds going back to the Civil War and the 'Skirmish of Belton'.

In the 19th century the park was regularly used by the Lincolnshire Yeomanry for exercises and the 3rd Earl was appointed their commander in chief. In the Second World War Belton Park was used by the RAF Regiment, but it was during the First World War that it played a crucial military role.

Left This photo shows part of the camp barracks and the temporary branch line from the East Coast mainline to Belton Park

## The First World War

At the outbreak of war in 1914, the 3rd Earl Brownlow offered the War Department the use of Belton Park. This offer was readily accepted and Belton Park was used by the British Expeditionary Force before becoming the training school for the newly formed Machine Gun Corps. Initially just a tented village, the camp soon grew with the addition of barracks, chapels, post offices, water towers, school rooms, YMCA huts and a camp hospital.

Between 1915 and 1922, around 175,000 men would spend six weeks training at Belton before being posted to the Western front, Mesopotamia (modern-day Iraq), Egypt, Palestine, Russia, Italy, Greece, India or East Africa.

## New research

Remains of the camp can still be seen around Bellmount Wood. We are currently working with members of the 'Old Comrades Association' of the MGC to further our understanding of what happened at Belton during 1915–22 and would be interested in hearing from anyone who can help add to our understanding of this very different aspect of Belton's history.

INDIA — N.W.RUSSIA
E. AFRICA — EGYPT
SALONIKA — ITALY
PALESTINE — MESOPOTAMIA
FRANCE — BELGIUM
1915–22
THE MACHINE GUN CORPS

Don't be Alarmed! the BELTON BOYS. are "On Guard."

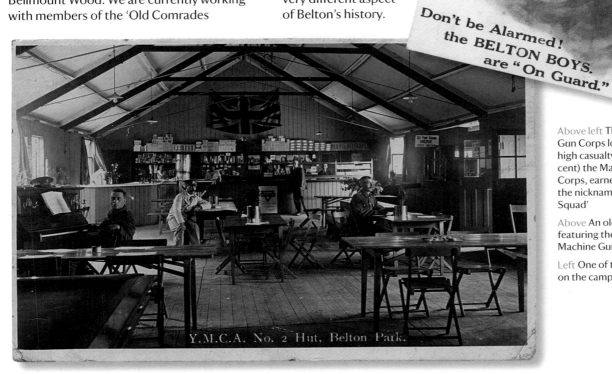

Y.M.C.A. No. 2 Hut, Belton Park.

Above left The Machine Gun Corps logo. Due to its high casualty rate (50 per cent) the Machine Gun Corps, earned themselves the nickname 'Suicide Squad'

Above An old postcard featuring the Belton Machine Gun Corps

Left One of the YMCA huts on the camp

# The Wider Estate

## The model village

Belton village is a wonderful example of a model village and was given conservation area status in 1985. It features buildings designed by Jeffry Wyatville (who also designed the Orangery in the Italian garden) and Anthony Salvin (who designed the Boathouse). It included cottages for estate workers, almshouses, a school, forge, inn, village cross, miniature village green, pump obelisk, pigeoncote, sawmill and Home Farm. The buildings are constructed of coursed ashlar stone with slate roofs.

## The church

The parish church of Saints Peter and Paul is not part of the Belton estate or looked after by the National Trust. It does, however, have very close associations with the Brownlow family and contains memorials to Brownlows and Custs as well as a number of spectacular tomb sculptures.

Above The Church of Saints Peter and Paul, seen here from the Italian Garden, contains many memorials to members of the Brownlow and Cust families

Left A street in Belton, the picturesque estate village adjacent to Belton Park

Opposite The Lion Gates

### The Lion Gates

The lodge house was moved to its present site at the end of the mile-long drive in 1810 when the main road from Grantham to Lincoln was altered. The lions are actually the snow leopard supporters of Viscount Tyrconnel (the term 'supporters' is used to describe animals or mythical creatures featured on a coat of arms).

### Towthorpe village

Towthorpe was abandoned before the plague, but so far we do not know why it came to be deserted. All you can now see are archaeological remains and earthworks of this deserted medieval village.

### Surrounding villages

In addition to Belton, estate workers also lived in the neighbouring villages such as Manthorpe and Londonthorpe. In Manthorpe a distinctive rustic Jacobean style was used, houses were built in brick with exotic chimney stacks, steep stepped gables and pretty wooden porches and verandahs.

Originally built in the 12th century, the church you see today is the result of centuries of remodelling. It has medieval and Jacobean additions with a large part of the current church belonging to the early 19th century.

In 1816 the 1st Earl commissioned Wyatville to design a chapel to his late wife Sophia Hume. His work is particularly notable as it incorporates Canova's statue of 'Religion', the only statue by this great Italian sculptor to exist in an English parish church. Wyatville also refaced the north wall and is thought to have added the west door in the tower, the roof pinnacles and crenellations. The pews were later installed by the 3rd Earl in 1891.

# Servants at Belton

Right The Old Kitchen

Below left Door plate to the Old Kitchen

Below Servants' bells in the Basement

Over the years following the First World War the world changed dramatically with rapid advances in technology and greater mechanisation. The number of people employed in service dropped to around 300,000 and many areas of the large country house estates became redundant or derelict.

## Below stairs

Unfortunately, Belton has very little information about the people who worked in the house or on the estate and very few items or records remain.

At the beginning of the 20th century, over two million people in Britain were employed in service. In the 19th century, Lord Brownlow had homes in London, Cheshire and Hertfordshire; he usually only visited Belton in the spring and so staffing levels changed depending on whether the family were in residence.

As with most large houses male and female servants were often kept apart. At Belton, the below stairs area was divided by a passage that runs the full length of the basement. As a rule, the rooms on one side were used by the female servants (such as the Housekeeper's Room and the Still Room) whilst those on the other were used by the male servants (for instance the Butler's Pantry and the beer cellars).

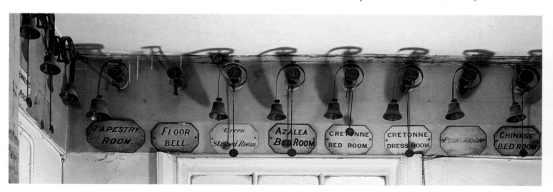

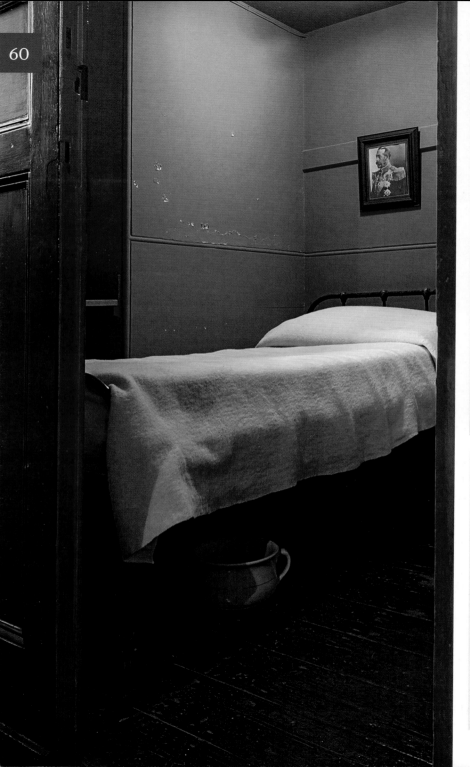

### The Beer Cellar

This is a much bigger storage area than the Wine Cellar next door. Servants' wages contained a beer allowance and so much beer was needed that it was brewed and barrelled on site in the Brewhouse (now the National Trust shop).

The daily allocation of beer was as follows:

| Male servants | Female servants |
| --- | --- |
| 1 pint at Lunch | ½ pint at Lunch |
| 1 pint at Dinner | 1 pint at Dinner |
| 1 pint at Supper | ½ pint at Supper |

If you missed a meal due to work your beer was kept for you, although your meal probably wasn't.

Above In the mid-19th century the Wine Cellar would have been stocked with about 5,000 wine bottles

Above right A handy hoist on the Servants' Staircase

Opposite The Under Butler's sparsely furnished bedroom in the Basement

## The Housekeeper's Room

The Housekeeper's Room was also known as 'the Pug's Parlour' (Pug was a nickname for the upper servants). This was where the Housekeeper did her accounts, stored the best china and linen and managed the House Maids.

## The Butler's Pantry

This room was used by the Butler to manage the business of the house. From here he also controlled access to the best glass, silver, wine and beer, all of which were in his care and stored close by.

## The Tunnel

During the late 1860s the Kitchen was connected to the main house by a tunnel. It was used to move items such as food, laundry and coal, but it was also a way by which servants could move from the house to the other domestic offices without being seen.

## The Wine Cellar

Inventories show that in 1857 the Wine Cellar contained 413 dozen bottles of wine (more than 4,900 bottles). This amazing collection included 120 bottles of champagne and 120 bottles of claret. In addition, the cellar also contained numerous bottles of Madeira, sherry and port. This area was the preserve of the Butler, who would pour the bottles into cut-glass decanters for the dining table. It is likely that the Butler would hold the only key to this room; it is reported that in many houses, the lock would also be sealed with wax!

# Belton Today

First-time visitors are often surprised by the scale of Belton, expecting a much smaller property. There is so much to see and do and our presentation is constantly evolving, that we welcome back an increasing number of returning visitors each year.

A lot has happened at Belton since the property came to the National Trust in 1984. An ongoing programme of conservation across the estate has seen the restoration of the Boathouse and the Orangery, the reintroduction of the Statue Walk, Cascade and a maze. The park is now being looked after following a programme of parkland management, which includes the restoration of the deer herd, increased protection for species such as the white-clawed crayfish and a range of archaeological surveys.

Meanwhile, in the house, the Red Drawing Room has been redecorated and the Blue Bedroom restored, while the Hondecoeter paintings in the Dining Room and the wonderful lapis cabinet have been conserved. But these are just the tip of the iceberg of our conservation work.

Visitors enjoying the house and gardens, clockwise from right:
on Belton House steps, outside the Orangery, in the playground, a volunteer helping with gardening

## Acknowledgements

The author has drawn on previous editions of the guidebook by Adrian Tinniswood and would also like to thank Andrew Barber (Curator), Carl Hawke (Wildlife & Countryside Consultant), David Fitzer (Conservation Manager), Catherine Granger (House & Collections Manager), Chris Shaw (Head Warden) and Jon Lawrence (Head Gardener).

## Illustrations

Alamy/Heritage Image Partnership Ltd p.21 (left); Alamy/travelib prime p.56 (left); Bridgeman Art Library p.21 (right); Corbis/ Heritage Images pp.32–33; Corbis/Michael Nicholson p.6 (bottom right); Edmund Fairfax-Lucy © front cover; FLPA/Derek Middleton p.53 (top right); RIBA p.40 (bottom); National Trust/Rika Gordon pp.48–49, p.50, p.52; National Trust/Gary Morgan p.8, p.57 (bottom); National Trust Images p.9 (bottom right), p.13 (right), p.17 (top and bottom) p.18, p.20 (left and right), pp.22–23, p.24 (left and right), p.30, p.31, p.33 (bottom), p.35, p.40 (top), p.47 (top); National Trust Images/Andrew Butler pp.2–3, p.44, National Trust Images/Brian and Nina Chapple p.41, pp.46–47 (top); National Trust Images/Andreas von Einsiedel p.1, p.9 (left), p.10 (left), p.23 (top), p.25 (top), p.59;

National Trust Images/Mark Fiennes p.16, p.45 (bottom), back cover; National Trust Images/ Roy Fox p.7 (left), p.13 (left), p.26, p.27, p.37 (right), p.39 (top); National Trust Images/ Dennis Gilbert p.15 (bottom right), p.22 (left), p.58 (bottom), pp.60–61 (all); National Trust Images/John Hammond p.4 (left), p.7 (right), p.9 (top right), p.12, p.15 (top), p.19 (top), p.23 (bottom), p.25 (bottom), p.29 (top), p.32 (left and right), p.34, p.58 (top); National Trust Images/Jack Heath p.39 (right), p.47 (bottom); National Trust Images/Robert Morris p.29 (bottom); National Trust Images/Megan Taylor pp.4–5, p.5 (right), p.43, p.45 (top), p.46 (bottom), pp.50–51, pp.56–57, p.62, p.63 (all); National Trust Images/Robert Thrift pp.10–11, p.36, p.37 (left); National Trust Images/Rupert Truman p.11 (right); National Trust Images/ Rachel Warne p.19 (bottom); National Trust Images/Bat Conservation Trust/Hugh Clark p.53 (top left); National Trust Images/NaturePL/ Andy Sands p.53 (bottom right).

## The National Trust

is a registered charity

is independent of government

was founded in 1895 to preserve places of historic interest or natural beauty permanently for the benefit of the nation

protects and opens to the public over 350 historic houses, gardens and parks, ancient monuments and nature reserves

owns nearly 250,000 hectares (618,000 acres) of the most beautiful countryside and almost 750 miles of outstanding coastline for people to enjoy

relies on the generosity of its supporters through membership subscriptions, gifts, legacies and the contribution of many tens of thousands of volunteers.

If you would like to become a member or make a donation, please telephone 0344 800 1895 (minicom 0344 800 4410); write to National Trust, PO Box 574, Rotherham S63 3FH; or visit our website at www.nationaltrust.org.uk

Text by Claire Cavendish
Edited by Claire Masset
Bird's-eye view by Simon Roulstone
Designed by Mike Blacker

Printed by Acorn Press, Swindon, for National Trust (Enterprises) Ltd, Heelis, Kemble Drive, Swindon, Wilts SN2 2NA on Cocoon Silk made from 100% recycled paper

Why not stay in a National Trust holiday cottage and explore other sites in the area? Call 0344 800 2070, or visit
**www.nationaltrustcottages.co.uk**

Clumber Park

Stainsby Mill

Hardwick Hall

The Workhouse

Belton House

Grantham House

Woolsthorpe Manor

© Maps in Minutes/Collins Bartholomew 2014